GW00401243

TIPPY'S STORY

LUCY POSTGATE

Grosvenor House
Publishing Limited

This book is published by
Grosvenor House Publishing Ltd
Link House
140 The Broadway, Tolworth, Surrey, KT6 7HT.
www.grosvenorhousepublishing.co.uk

A CIP record for this book
is available from the British Library

ISBN 978-1-83975-453-1

Also available:

Storm's Story
Miranda's Story

Chapter One

Why would anyone want a Quarter Horse when they could have a whole horse?

That is the sort of stupid thing I might have said before I got to know one. In my ignorance, I thought a Quarter Horse was like a Tennessee Walking Horse or Yankee Doodles Pony – an odd sort of horse, special to America, with a bit of a silly name.

It is good to be proved wrong every now and again.

Living in Britain, we all know about Thoroughbred horses, New Forest ponies, Shetland ponies, Fells, Dales and many more of our native breeds, but there is not much said about the breed known as the American Quarter Horse.

This is odd, as the Quarter Horse is not only the most popular horse in the USA, but it is also exported and bred all over the globe, including Britain. There are more than three million Quarter Horses registered worldwide – which means there are a lot of them about.

And fifteen years on, I can confirm what all those horse owners already know; that there are very many reasons why you might want an American Quarter Horse.

Alanna was fast outgrowing her beloved Welsh Mountain pony, Miranda, so we were tentatively looking for another horse, maybe something we could both ride? A Quarter Horse had not been particularly on my mind, but there was a recommended one for sale.

Tippy was waiting for us, all plump and polite with the big doe eyes of a youngster and an inquisitive expression on her face. She stood nearly 15 hands high and had been washed and groomed until her dark bay coat gleamed in the sunlight. She was five years old and had been well fed and well handled.

We were first shown her paces in a round pen before being allowed to ride. Not only was an American Quarter Horse new to me, but so was a round pen. It was like a large round cage. I am used to lunging horses for exercise and training. The round pen worked the same – a bit like lunging, but without the rein. The pen was bigger than 20-metres diameter and Tippy could walk, trot, canter and change direction. She was obedient to the voice commands and did not do anything crazy.

Alanna had a quick sit up on her – only walking and trotting. We liked the mare.

I am always cautious when buying a horse.

My first questions being, 'Why are you selling this horse? Why don't you want to keep her for yourself?'

Happily, Tippy was owned by my long-standing horsey friend Ro, so I knew exactly why Tippy was for sale.

Ro has owned and bred many horses. She bought Tippy as an untrained youngster to bring on and use for herself. Ro does carriage driving as well as riding, so she was hoping Tippy would do both. Long before Alanna and I went to meet Tippy, Ro had entertained me with hilarious stories about teaching Tippy to drive. This is done with two long reins attached to the horse and the person some distance behind holding the said reins, giving the appropriate commands. Ro would take Tippy on the long reins around the farm. Tippy was intelligent and biddable. That is, until she saw what she thought was something scary ahead. It could be the water trough, or the harrows that had been left in the same field for months, or just the wind making patterns in the wheat. Tippy's extra fast 180-degree turn would come in to play. Ro would be left with a cat's cradle of reins and her horse looking straight at her, the mare rolling her eyes in horror.

Lots of horses and ponies take to being driven well, some prefer pulling to being ridden. Tippy was not one of them. It did not take many more sliding stops, one-eighties and Tippy hysterics for Ro to untangle the reins one last time and write her off as a driving horse.

So, there you have it, a good reason for the sale, plus an additional bonus that Alanna and I could take Tippy on a month trial before agreeing to the purchase. Ro also agreed to deliver her. No prospective purchase can be fairer than that.

Tippy's arrival was delayed by a couple of weeks. It was late October when we had gone to meet her and, Lewes being Lewes, Ro and I agreed to leave delivery until after Bonfire night. November fifth is the biggest, noisiest date in the Lewes town calendar. The run-up to Bonfire night begins in September with firework displays and processions taking place around the county every weekend. The biggest and best happens in Lewes on the fifth. None of this is horse-friendly, of course, but I think animals that have lived here for years get used to the bangs and flashes to a certain extent. Perhaps mine are particularly lucky that we live a short way out of the town. Either way, it was not appropriate to welcome Tippy to her new life with fireworks and flaming torches.

During the waiting time, I decided to educate myself about this breed known as the American Quarter Horse. The more I researched, the more interested I became.

The Quarter Horse is the oldest surviving American horse breed. They were developed by crossing the native Chickasaw Indian pony with the Thoroughbred horse. The odd name comes from the horse's ability to gallop at extreme speed over the distance of a quarter of a mile. Over that short sprint, the Quarter Horse would even beat a Thoroughbred, the current record for a Quarter Horse being just over 20 seconds from a standing start. That is fast.

The Chickasaw pony genes gave the horse the powerful shoulders and hindquarters which enable the breed to carry a full-grown wrangler, a loaded-up Western saddle and possibly the odd calf. The breed also inherited an instinct for working with cattle. I have more recently spoken to people who have worked on cattle ranches in California and Montana, and they all agree the Quarter Horse knows how to cut, turn, stop, gallop and herd without being told, a bit like a Collie dog. Now I am sure those skills did not come from the Thoroughbred.

Eventually, the day was set. Tippy would arrive at lunchtime on Saturday. I gave my usual morning riding school lessons while Alanna stayed at the farm perfecting Tippy's stable bedding and adding a welcome pack of fresh water, sweet meadow hay and a carrot.

At exactly the designated hour, the Land Rover, trailer, Ro and Tippy rolled into our yard. Tippy had travelled for three hours without a break, but she unloaded without a bead of sweat on her body. She was amazing – totally chilled – the best traveller I have ever come across.

Tippy peered around her new home. Every horse in the yard was leaning over the stable door or craning over the paddock wall to get a better look at the new girl. There was much high blowing and snorting as Alanna gave her a brief tour of the premises.

So many new friends to greet! Tippy met Dylan, otherwise known as The King. He was my first pony and the start of it all, now a wise, respected, elderly Welsh Mountain pony. Next door, Ottie, a grey Thoroughbred and the most beautiful horse in the world, watched Tippy with interest – a possible rival in the camp? Then there was bossy Bug the New Forest pony and little Lobelia, the Shetland pony, two opinionated chestnut mares. In the pony field, Miranda and her three-year-old daughter Mia, both Welsh Mountain ponies, were trotting up and down, wanting a bit of the action. In the furthest stable lived Killin, a good-looking bay Thoroughbred cross Irish Draught mare. She greeted Tippy with squeals of delight. Killin always had a lot to say.

Once Tippy had said hello to her new neighbours, she was allowed into her stable next door to Killin. She began as she has continued, tucking into her hay with a healthy appetite.

Ro had brought Tippy's documents and a loan agreement for us both to sign. Tippy's real name on her passport is Kir Royale. Kir Royale is a cocktail made from champagne and crème de cassis. She was therefore nicknamed Tipsy (too many cocktails), but this had quickly become Tippy.

There was also a big bundle of papers showing Tippy's pedigree as a foundation mare. Foundation stock have less Thoroughbred in their breeding, only about 16%, than some more modern Quarter Horses. They are considered by some purists to be the only 'true' Quarter Horses. A high percentage of tough little Chickasaw pony seems like a good idea to me.

Chapter Two

Knowing that Tippy had a vivid imagination and saw scary things in hedges and around corners, we began her training here with gentle rides out, accompanied by a sensible older horse. This usually meant me on Killin or Ottie, and Alanna on Tippy. It was fun, and Alanna and Tippy seemed to like each other right from the start. Alanna bought her purple accessories and a glittery 'Princess Tippy' browband. We happily paid the money over to Ro, and Tippy joined our family.

Inconveniently, Alanna had to go to school five days a week. This left me as the main rider for Tippy.

Any direction we ride from our home in the South Downs, we come across a steep hill. This makes for well-muscled, strong, balanced horses. Going up the hill on Tippy was fine. She powered her way up as if we were climbing the Rockies. Coming back down was a whole new experience for me – quite different from the neat Thoroughbred types that I am used to.

Tippy carried her head low, tucked her hindquarters underneath her body and slid her way down the path as if her hooves were on four skis. It was an alarming experience.

She also liked life on the edge. On the few paths round here with a steep drop on one side, she would always gravitate towards the edge of the precipice. I do not know why she did it. Was it fun? Or was the going just slightly better on the skinny edge of the path?

Occasionally I found myself so near the edge of something I decided it was best not to interfere, for fear of making the situation more dangerous. It was quite a lesson in keeping calm and sitting still, though in fact, she never got it wrong. Maybe the Chickasaw pony in her yearned for the challenge of a narrow mountain trail.

I had to draw the line at walking into bushes and trees by mistake. Tippy was interested in absolutely everything – it could be a deer, a clump of unusual foliage or another horse in the distance. She would fix her eyes on whatever had taken her attention and keep on walking. In the beginning, I trusted her not to walk into things, but after I had untangled us from brambles and picked blackthorns from my face a few times, I took control more seriously.

Tippy was remarkably comfortable. She was always enthusiastic, with a lovely long stride and an almost squashy, springy back.

The first few winter months of her life here were uneventful. Short days and poor weather meant we did not ask too much of her. January and February are always slow months in the riding school.

Sometime in the early spring I was riding Tippy alone as usual. A group of mostly Thoroughbred horses and assorted dogs from the riding school next door caught up with me. We continued riding out together, nattering about the usual stuff, the weather, the dogs and my new horse.

When we got to the gate into a wonderful open space of grassland known as the Battle of Lewes Land, I really should have turned for home. I did not. We all went through. Most of the riding school and all the dogs took off at a gallop. I felt Tippy hesitate for a second. Then she turned into a bronco. She did three or four of the most enormous bucks that I have ever tried to sit on, her head between her knees and a few twists thrown in.

Crashing to the ground, I managed to keep hold of her reins so at least she did not show the Thoroughbreds her extreme speed as well.

"You should have had a neck strap," said my friend from the riding school as she cantered off to catch up with the others.

I walked Tippy home feeling very bruised and battered, mulling on whether a narrow strap around Tippy's neck would really have helped me stay on. I doubt it. But I was mostly cross with myself for expecting my youngster to behave in that situation.

Quarter Horses are famous for being one of the most versatile horse breeds in the world. They can race, show jump, travel long distances, do dressage, herd cattle and perform rodeo amongst other things.

I guess if you buy a potential bronco, you are likely to get a bronco.

*   *   *

Tippy's youth and inexperience was evident in another painful experience during that early spring – this time painful for Tippy, not me.

Our cottage and stables are on a farm. A hundred years ago, like many farms in Sussex, it was a busy sheep farm. In the mid-twentieth century, the farm changed to arable, with just a few cattle. Most of our own field fencing is horse-friendly post and rail, but inevitably, on a farm, there is barbed wire.

Tippy had spent the day out in the field with her friend Bug. Miranda and Mia were there too, but, mother and daughter, happy in their own company, generally stayed away from Tippy and Bug. The native ponies live out in the field all year round. Tippy needed to come into the stable at night, so I went to collect her at tea-time.

Horror of horrors! Half of Tippy's face skin was hanging off. Her baby-soft skin covered in dark bay hair had literally been sliced off the right-hand side of her face. It was still attached in places. She must have put her head through the wire fence to try and reach some grass, and then pulled back carelessly. Tippy was grotesque and in terrible pain. Our poor beautiful horse.

The vet was brilliant. She arrived quickly and immediately gave Tippy pain relief and a sedative. To this day, I remain in awe of that vet. She spent a long time cleaning the wounds. When I thought she had got the face as clean as it could possibly be, she carried on cleaning. When she finally thought her work was good enough, the wounds were not stitched but stapled.

Expertly, the vet used eight staples to reattach the skin to the head. It was a work of art. Already the dreadful torn face was beginning to look like a horse again.

Eighteen months later there was barely a scar. Today, visually, you would not know the accident had ever happened.

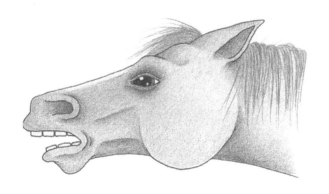

Chapter Three

Tippy had a course of antibiotics and a boring week in the stable. Two weeks after the accident, the same vet called in to take out the staples. She approached the stable ahead of me. Tippy flew at her across the box, ears flat back and teeth snapping. Whoa! We beat a hasty retreat.

Tippy is an intelligent and sensitive horse and remembered exactly how much pain she had been in last time she met this vet. It was a sad day.

With the help of a little more sedation, Tippy was unstapled. The healing of the face continued well. The trauma to Tippy's temperament was not so good.

The vet visit was the first time I ever saw Tippy attack anyone. However, looking back over the few months that she had lived with us, she had shown some signs of hostility. There was no one thing, but various awkward little irritations.

She would snap her teeth when the front of her rug was being buckled. Tummy straps and hind leg straps were no problem.

Her back twitched when she was saddled, particularly when I straightened the saddle pad on her withers.

She ground her teeth when the girth was tightened, however gently it was done.

Grooming her chest and between her front legs was a hazard.

She had become difficult picking up her front hooves. She would stretch her leg forwards, lock her knee, saying, 'Nope. It is not possible. It won't bend.'

Tippy had been trained with a reward of a mint for good behaviour, but when she did not get her mint, and I am not in the habit of giving treats from the hand, it was ears back and gnashing teeth.

What she hated most of all was people leaning on the door and looking in at her. She would stand and make horrible mare faces – warning you out of her personal space.

If you persisted in 'looking at her' (how dare you?) she would come at you with teeth bared.

She acquired a new stable name – Nippy Tippy.

When Tippy was not being irritated by us humans, she was a delight. She was a beautiful mare, her soft and silky coat quite different from the other residents. She looked like she was just waiting to be stroked and cuddled.

Beware – looks deceive!

Over the decades, I have watched some horse owners deal with horses who are sore, sour or scared. Or all those things. Their approach is to show the horse 'who is boss' with harsh words, heavy hands and a variety of 'training aids'. I have done it myself until I knew better. It is how we were taught in the 1970s.

Long term, those methods do not work.

Horses are not born nasty – there had to be reasons why she was unhappy. She was trying to tell us something.

Rather than confront her nastiness, I tried the avoid and ignore routine. If your child or toddler (or your horse, for that matter) is having a bit of a paddy, there is nothing worse than being ignored.

My carefully placed elbow wedged in Tippy's neck stopped her teeth getting anywhere near me when doing her rug or brushing her chest.

Distraction and surprise generally worked for the girth.

The hoof picking was different. Your leg will not bend? So, I ask you to step backwards. It worked a treat.

I ignored her scary mare faces when I was mucking out her stable. Sometimes I would hear a clunking, grinding noise close behind me, but I continued to work around her and always got the job done.

I did not shout or growl at her, I simply took no notice. It must have been very annoying for her.

If Tippy had really wanted to hurt me, she could have done. I do not think she wanted to make contact – she was trying to communicate in the best way she knew how. I hoped to understand her and build up her trust.

As a yearling, Tippy had won prizes on the showing circuit. Perhaps the posing, fussing and standing four-square for hours on end, had soured her a bit. Or maybe there were just too many opinionated judges discussing her faults. No one would like that.

At some point, there probably had been some damage to Tippy's withers, as the saddle continued to be tricky. A new saddle and regular visits from the chiropractor helped considerably. She did not look uncomfortable or object to being ridden, but to this day, she has tickly withers. These days if you want her to be your best friend, give her withers a good scratch. She will love you forever. Or at least she will love you until you stop scratching and want to pick out her hooves.

A sad fact is that the few people who have felt Tippy's actual teeth on their flesh are those who love her best.

Alanna was leading her to the field one day with a slice of haylage under the other arm when Tippy went for a bite of the haylage and found Alanna's tummy instead. Okay, maybe it was a misjudgement, but Alanna has some impressive tooth marks on her tummy.

Another rider who adores Tippy managed to get her face bitten because she tried to take a snatched geranium plant out of Tippy's mouth. Was Tippy just trying to keep hold of the geranium? Who knows, but it still should not have happened. Happily, this time there were no permanent teeth marks.

There are a few people who Nippy Tippy really wants to savage.

The horse chiropractor was high on her hit list. It takes a lot of pressure to release those knotted tissues and treatment can be painful for the patient. Tippy blamed the chiropractor for every ache or pain she had ever had and began snapping and grinding her teeth as soon as the poor chiropractor walked into the yard. We had to resort to putting a grazing muzzle on her while she was being treated. She could snap away loudly, letting us know exactly what she thought of us, but not make contact. Over the months, Tippy became less sore and therefore less ferocious. Eventually, I only had to carry the pink muzzle on my shoulder for Tippy to keep her teeth to herself. We have dispensed with the muzzle now, but Tippy has a long memory and I am always there to hold and distract her during treatments.

As for the licencing vet, he dared to prod her lumbar region hard, without asking first. She could not bite because I was holding her, so she took a good swing at him with a hind leg.

"If she had made contact, she would be struck off the list!" he told me sharply.

This vet only comes every other year to inspect my horses for the riding school licence. Tippy knows it is him straight away and is immediately on the defensive. Maybe I am too? Nobody likes to be inspected.

Obviously, I could not have Tippy gnashing her teeth at my clients and friends. I put a sign on her door reading – Do Not Approach. I May Bite.

You would think that was clear enough.

Human nature being what it is, if we see a sign which tells us NOT to do something, the more we want to do it. Just to see what happens...

You would be amazed how many people saw the sign, read it, and then went to lean on Tippy's door and peer in like she was an animal in a zoo. Poor Tippy.

Chapter Four

Temperament issues aside, Tippy was a fun horse. She liked being ridden and she liked learning new things. She enjoyed being ridden in company and she was happy alone. True to the Quarter Horse reputation, she would have a go at anything.

When she was taught something new, she did her best to grasp it and was then keen to show off her new skills next day. Sometimes she could not wait to be asked – her working trot would turn into a long striding medium trot or a square halt would become a rein back – all without any input from the rider.

Later in life, she became so in tune with what the rider was thinking. One of my favourite games was to see how many movements Tippy and I could do, using thought waves alone. The answer is lots!

One time I was teaching a pupil on Tippy to ride a walk pirouette. I explained exactly how to approach this turn on the spot, what aids to use and where to carry out the pirouette in the school. Tippy is also impatient and wants to get on with the job. Clearly, I was talking too much. Tippy and rider set off. At exactly the appointed place, Tippy performed a 180-degree pirouette and trotted away in the other direction. My rider may have been thinking it, but she had not begun to give the commands. My rider was astonished and Tippy was pleased with herself.

Although Tippy is ridden English style in the riding school, she is perfectly amiable to have a go at being a

Western horse. She enjoys being ridden with one hand only, on long reins. Her Western jog is a joy – so slow and comfy we could keep going for miles. I admit we never perfected the long, slow, relaxed canter known as the lope. We did try, but Tippy's canter is always a bit too exciting. Racing around barrels and sliding stops are fantastic though. As is her standing start to gallop – she is the horse version of a Ferrari.

Tippy's ability to turn into a Western horse is great for hacking. She will change her mood to suit the situation – she can be speedily chasing off predators or dozing under the lonesome pine tree.

If she is having a slow ride with Storm, the Welsh cob who joined the yard in 2009, then slow and sleepy it is – the slow jog coming into play and maybe a semblance of a lope.

A different day and a different mood, you could well be chasing coyote.

In the early years when she was ridden out with Ottie, there was always a competitive edge. I never let either of them go 'full throttle'. I am not a race rider. The fastest I have ever galloped was on Ottie in a mock hunt years ago. A mock hunt is riders chasing after another rider who has set off in advance wearing a colourful sash. It was a slightly misty morning with poor visibility on the hills above Newhaven. Ottie was so fast I could not see a thing. Quite terrifying, really. I loved Tippy and Ottie dearly – I did not need to know who was the fastest over a quarter-mile or two miles, or four miles for that matter.

When Tippy was ridden out with Miranda, the little pony who wanted to be a racehorse, there was always an unexpected race involved. However calmly and quietly I tried to escort a hack from my calm place on Killin, I would regularly see Tippy and Miranda disappearing off into the distance. Neither of them was going to give in. It was bad-mannered, awful training and I was not proud of their behaviour. My clients loved them.

Alanna took to doing some dressage on Tippy. I have said before that Tippy's canter is not her greatest pace. Walk, trot, gallop, yes – not canter. Competitive dressage was never going to be our most important thing. That said, one sunny summer show, Alanna had completed a good test, but things were running late. Horse and parents were fractious and looking to get home. There was just a chance Alanna and Tippy might be placed. If not, we really wanted to get home.

An idea came to us. Tim had brought his long lens camera with him. He sidled up to the Range Rover where the judge was sitting, zoomed in over the judge's shoulder and took a clear picture of the score sheet. Not the most conventional way to check your score, I am sure, but Tippy left with a big, navy rosette attached to her bridle.

As an adult, I had many riding lessons at Ditchling Common Stud until the school sadly closed some years ago. I loved it. There is always more to learn. As well as being a British Horse Society approved centre and teaching all the usual stuff, the school had an international Skill at Arms team. My teacher commented on what a good Skill at Arms horse Tippy would be – fast gallop, straight lines and quick stops. Alanna had a few lessons on DCS Skill at Arms horses. She was good – slicing oranges on hooks at a gallop and stabbing hessian sacks full of straw. The one reined riding practice had been good training. Why not try it at home?

Tippy takes to most things. She can do the 0 to 55mph start and stop in a straight line. We had made a weapon out of a broom handle and a nail to go 'tent pegging'. The rider gallops up the line of tent pegs, weapon in hand, and endeavours to pick up as many pegs as possible. So far so good – except Tippy could not cope with the weapon and peg being swept up past her right eye. She had to leap sideways every time. And I mean every time. It got a bit silly. After Alanna had made a few too many unexpected dismounts, we decided Skill at Arms could go the same way as carriage driving. Tippy was not cut out for combat either.

Show jumping and cross-country jumping were fun. Tippy had speed, enthusiasm and ability, although I will admit, she would never have made a show jumper. Tippy has always felt she knows best about everything, and if the rider faced her at an obstacle which she felt needed investigating first, she could have a serious attack of trembly legs before jumping from a standstill or worse, perform the sliding stop and sit down. Recently one of my pupils ended up slowly slithering into a ditch, as Tippy stared down at the abyss, legs wobbling, unable to take off. Her frights were never at the jump which one would expect her to dislike. It would be something stupid like poles with sunlight glinting on them, or the teensy, weensy ditch. Then she would go right on and clear a spooky table or a bath full of water and plastic ducks.

There were other aspects of living with Tippy that we had to get used to.

I took two pupils to a cross-country practice locally. One girl was on Tippy, the other on her own horse. It was a warm, slightly humid day on a lovely farm with many different sizes and shapes of jumps. It should have been such fun. The girls had only jumped a couple of fences when we were set upon by dozens of horse flies – big and brown with huge eyes and fangs. They all went straight for delicious Tippy. We had fly sprayed both horses and we tried to swat the flies away, but to no effect. Tippy was beside herself. Her skin quivered and she trembled. She tried to rub herself on the other horse and on me. She almost got down to roll. She sweated and frothed and neighed out to me. The horse flies loved her even more. They swarmed!

There was only one thing to do – we all headed fast back to the horse trailer, slapping many dead as we ran. We loaded up and went home. What a disappointment.

Tippy was not being naughty. She was genuinely acutely affected by the flies. Her skin was covered in lumps where she had been bitten. The other horse, hardly at all.

Another time Tippy was to have some acupuncture treatment. I held her head while the therapist placed multiple needles along her back and on her shoulders. All the needles in place, we stepped back to wait for them to work their magic. Tippy immediately shook herself hard from head to hoof. All the needles sprayed off her, landing on the floor.

Acupuncture does not hurt, although there is a bit of a strange 'sensation' at the site of the needle. Tippy could not even cope with this.

I think both incidents taught us a lot about Tippy, her extreme sensitivity and therefore, her alleged bad temper.

Chapter Five

One summer, after some mighty preparation, Tim, George, Alanna and I went on a holiday, which became known as our Great American Road Trip. It was my treat – something I had wanted to do for years. I organised the trip and planned our route and destinations.

We flew to San Francisco where we picked up a huge, four-litre Ford Edge, which we drove from the coast of California to the Yosemite National Park 10,000 feet above sea level. We took in the most incredible rocky landscape and spectacular views seen from high winding roads speckled with the last bits of snow, even though it was June. We chomped on dried papaya and salt-water taffy.

Leaving California, we drove on through Nevada. There is no one in Nevada. We took the Interstate 80. It is not the famous 'Loneliest road in America', but the next one up. We rarely saw another vehicle. When we did, it was either a monster American Trucker truck bearing down on us at speed, or we were overtaken by a massive Dodge pick-up truck with a sheep standing up in the back looking down on us from above our eye level. We realised then that we were not in a huge 4x4 at all, just an ordinary little runabout by American standards.

The roads were completely straight and looked to go on forever. With a speed limit of 85mph, cruise control and the road to ourselves, we covered the miles fast. At one point we found ourselves driving alongside a railway train with 121 carriages. It was an extraordinary sight as we all raced along. Back in England, you are lucky if you get four carriages on a train to London.

There is a family joke that wherever I go on holiday, it rains. Wales, Portugal, Scotland, France – it rains while I am there. I try and dispute this sometimes, but let me tell you, driving across the empty, barren Nevada desert, where the temperature gauge in the Ford at one point reached 100 degrees Fahrenheit, it rained! Extraordinary, heavy rain, turning to steam as it hit the hot road. All my fault, of course.

Eventually, we left the gloomy roads of Nevada with their State prisons, Native American Indian reservations and huge advertising billboards and drove on into more prosperous Idaho.

Our journey through southern Idaho was dominated by the silvery Snake River which literally snakes across the landscape. We met a lot more traffic and passed smart homesteads with crops and well-irrigated fields.

In the time that we had set aside for our road trip, we were never going drive across America, but we did cover four of the fifty states and drove well over two thousand miles.

Four days into our trip, we reached Montana and my dream destination. I drove us into West Yellowstone full of joy, feeling as if I was arriving home. I have always said I was born two hundred years too late.

West Yellowstone is a bustling Western town. There were bars with real swinging doors, shops selling outdoor wear, leatherwork and horse stuff. All ages of folk were wearing boots and Stetsons. We did not actually see horses tethered outside a saloon bar, but they were sure to have been there somewhere.

As a young kid, all I wanted was a pony, a cowboy hat and a cap gun. My pacifist parents did not think any of these things appropriate. I was given dolls like all other little girls.

When I grew up, I got myself a pony. I married a man with a gun. Now I was in the right place for the Stetson. So many outfitters, so much choice. I picked a black fold-up hat called a Minnetonka. I even rode out in it. The whole time we were in Montana, I only saw one rider wearing a traditional hard hat and he was a sullen young lad of about nine years old. I bet his parents were riding in their comfy wide-brimmed hats, keeping the sun off their noses.

We stayed in a log cabin at a ranch which was a mere stone's throw from Yellowstone National Park. There was no television, no internet in the cabins, no bar and no disco. The only sounds were birdsong, the running water of the Grayling Creek and coyote calling in the night. It was paradise!

Alanna and I went riding on the first morning. There were more than thirty equines on the ranch. They ranged from Quarter Horses to half-draughts, which are big and can carry a heavy American and mules. The mules will just follow the others apparently, which makes them good for beginners. The horses were saddled and tethered when we arrived at the stables. The wranglers checked us out for weight and ability. I was so hoping they did not take one look at me and put me on a half-draught or a mule...

In fact, I rode Raven, a beautiful, gentle Quarter Horse mare. Alanna rode Belle. The riding was stunning. We set off in bright sunshine along trails carpeted with blue, white, yellow and pink wild-flowers and bordered by aspen trees. Far in the distance were the snow-peaked Gallatin mountains. I have said before, in *Storm's Story*, but I am saying it again because I am still impressed, those Quarter Horses were so sure-footed and trustworthy. We rode up banks and down slopes, round things and over things, through dark forest and open plains. No spooking, no tripping, no fuss. We rode with no contact on the reins and let the horse take care of us. We felt very safe.

The horses were herded out to their pasture at night, all thirty of them, by the wranglers on horseback, and then herded in again in the morning. I asked about their diet, how did the ranch keep them so sane and sensible? The horses were fed almost exclusively on alfalfa (in the UK we call it lucerne) and grass. It was gratifying to know that my horses also live on the same food. Most days they are sane and sensible too.

Even the ranch horse training was not rushed in any way. There was a little palomino mare tethered to the fence. She was always there, not doing anything. I asked one of the wranglers, why?

"Being halter broke," was his reply. So chilled.

Riding Raven was similar to riding Tippy. She had that long, lolloping stride and flexible back, which made her especially comfortable. I can understand how working wranglers can spend days on end riding their Quarter Horses. But do not let anyone tell you that a Western saddle is more comfortable than an English one. It is not true. I had serious butt-ache after an hour. It was like sitting on a flat ironing board.

The ranch was heaven on earth for me. Not so much for our son. One evening the ranch had a cook-out which requires all the guests to ride to their supper. It was the only way you were going to get fed. As we lined up waiting to be allocated a horse, George was heard to say, "If these people knew about Facebook and the internet – this just wouldn't happen."

The cook-out was everything you would expect. Excellent food, cooked in the open air, cowboy beans (you have got to try real cowboy beans if you get the chance), fresh lemonade to drink and all accompanied by an old country singer and his guitar. He kept up songs and banter throughout. Much later, I was told he was not there only to entertain us. His job was to keep the wolves and bears away.

Wolves and bears like barbecue food and cowboy beans too. But not country and western music.

The ranch had a slow pace of life. I loved the peace and tranquillity of it. Nobody was looking at their phone worrying about deadlines or berating themselves for not being productive enough. The days were regulated by the weather and hours of daylight. Dot, the lady wrangler who escorted one of my rides out, had never been out of Montana. That sounds strange and unadventurous, but I could understand how it might be possible to stay happy forever in that Montana time warp.

However, our visit was short and our time was up. We roared back along those long, straight highways to the west coast and the noise and bustle of the real world. The airline pilot put his foot down, and with a following wind, we arrived home in England in record time.

Look out Tippy – we have plans for you!

Chapter Six

Returning to work in the riding school, I put on my hard hat and sensible boots. I gathered my rider registration forms, accident book and other documents that my UK licence requires. I went back to checking my wristwatch every ten minutes, running my lessons on time and took up my role as a responsible riding teacher. No leaning on the paddock fence in the Stetson and jeans over here.

The autumn following our Great American Road Trip, both George and Alanna left home for university. Of course, Tim and I missed them, but I did not get that thing called 'empty nest syndrome'. I was far too busy and besides, students return home, don't they? With their washing.

However, their absence did mean that the horse we had bought mostly for Alanna back in 2005 was now mostly mine. Happy days.

Tippy and I did a lot of hacking, with and without clients. It is what we both enjoy the most and she was more grown-up than when I had first ridden her. The best way to see the big outdoors is from the back of a horse – preferably a Quarter Horse.

She worked in the school with some of my pupils. She did not have the patience to be a novice rider's horse. She could not bear it if someone held the reins too tight, bumped about or worse, clamped their legs on her sides like a vice. She was irritated and uncomfortable and she showed it.

In a way, she had us just where she wanted us. She did not get the pupils on her back who were not ready. She did not have loads of adoring children around her wanting to stroke her and kiss her. Her beauty routine and health needs were seen to quickly and efficiently. She never had to suffer our busy, slightly chaotic Saturday afternoon Pony Care sessions. If Tippy was happy, she was a pleasure to be with.

A plan that I did not have for Tippy on our return from America was to have a foal from her. It was Tim's suggestion. For years he has questioned whether I need quite so many horses. For him to suggest breeding another one was quite out of character! I think his inner cowboy was surfacing.

He did not have to suggest it twice. With help from Ro, from whom I had purchased Tippy, we researched various Quarter Horse stallions. When I had bred Mia from Miranda, I had gone to the Welsh pony stud to look at the stallions. Now it was all done online. This gave us more choice, and as artificial insemination is increasingly popular, it meant we could look at stallions abroad too. I have never enjoyed working online. It is part of being born two hundred years too late. But Ro was good. If I came up with a video of a stallion which I thought looked promising, she could analyse, dissect the video and usually tell me I was wrong.

Eventually, we decided on a stallion who was recommended by Ro's farrier. Shiny Little Spark was the real deal. He was born in Mississippi in 1996, son of the famous Quarter Horse stallion, Shining Spark. He now lived at a Quarter Horse stud near Dartmoor. Sparky was a medal winner himself and had sired many prize-winning foals. He was also local enough for us to visit. We were pleased to be able to meet him and see some of his offspring.

Tim and I nipped down to Devon on the last day of April. Sparky was grazing in a field with two of his mares and their cute foals. The stud manager whistled for him and over he strolled. He stood at nearly 15-hands high, was bay, with a star and two white hind socks, the same markings as Tippy. He was a lighter bay than Tippy, physically bigger build and best of all, had a kind and friendly temperament. If it had been possible and ethical to clone Tippy, I would have done so. Sparky looked like he might produce another Tippy.

After touring the rest of the stud and chatting with the stud manager, we decided to book Tippy in for natural mating rather than AI. This meant Tippy would travel down to meet Sparky for a romantic holiday in Devon in the summer.

There were things to be done before she could go. Firstly, I had to ascertain precisely when she was coming into season. The plan would be to travel her down to the stud a week before coming into season. I did not want her away any longer than was necessary. She also needed a pre-breeding examination by the vet. The farrier removed her hind shoes too.

All was good. Her seasons were happening at regular intervals and the timing was right when Tippy began her journey to Devon in mid-June. She travelled in the comfort of a hired horse box with air conditioning and CCTV. I expected her back in a month.

Whether it was the stress of the journey or the torrential rain and strong winds that swept across the south-west on her arrival, I do not know, but Tippy did not come into season as planned.

She was grazing in paddocks by day and stabled at night, as at home. She got on well with another mare and thought Sparky was nice enough, but of no real interest. She was having the holiday of a lifetime. But no sex.

"She thinks she is on holiday camp!" messaged the stud manager.

The weeks went by. I kept in touch with the stud by email and text. Tippy was well and easy to handle, but still showed no sign of coming into season. As time was marching on and the breeding season was due to finish in August, Tippy was introduced to another stallion. Nope. Still not impressed.

We had the vet called to scan her. This revealed a 'stuck follicle' which was sorted by an injection of prostaglandin. She should have come into season three days later. Whether she did or not, Tippy still showed no interest in Sparky or the other chap. We were running out of time and would have to give up soon.

One evening at the beginning of August, Tippy was being brought in from the field into the big barns where the horses live at night. Tippy momentarily hesitated at Sparky's door. It was a flicker of interest which was picked up on. The sign of an excellent stud manager.

Romance blossomed. Love was in the air. During those hot August days, Tippy and Sparky finally got their act together.

Tippy did not come back into season. She had a positive pregnancy scan three weeks later and returned home to Sussex in early September. She had been away for nearly three months. Typical Tippy. Always suiting herself.

Chapter Seven

I have no objection to working a mare in the early stages of pregnancy and this is what I had planned to do with Tippy. What with her late return home from stud and appallingly heavy rain with strong winds here, it did not happen. We were battling against the elements most of that autumn, and there seemed no point getting her fit and ready, in order to turn her away again at Christmas. Tippy had spent the last three months on furlough – it looked like she would continue that way for the next eleven months. Maybe she had this planned all along?

Soon after her return home, the vet came to do another pregnancy scan. This is normal procedure to check she is still in foal and that she is not carrying twins. Twins in horses rarely survive. Tippy was sedated and scanned through the rectum. It was not straightforward. After about forty minutes of scanning and nothing to be seen, the vet was about to give up. She could not find a foal.

Disappointment hanging in the air, I rested my head on Tippy's damp, seal-like neck. I comforted myself that at least I had my mare safely back home and we would not have to go through this again. We could get on with life and work.

The vet, with determination and a very tired arm, had one more go with the ultrasound scanner.

Now you do not often hear a vet "whoop!" with joy, but that is exactly what she did. Tippy's twenty- eight-day-old baby was secretly tucked away, as far as possible, in the right-hand horn of her womb.

Yet another scan, a week later, showed an embryo and a beating heart. We allowed ourselves to get excited. Baby of Tippy was growing nicely.

*   *   *

Tippy was back out in the paddock with Bug, Storm, Miranda and Mia. They were known as the Fearsome Five. Not because any of them were vicious, they got on relatively well with each other. They were all, I would say, strong characters. Bug was the boss. Storm thought he should be boss but had not made the grade. Miranda knew she was too small to be boss, but that did not stop her challenging the big ones. Mia kept out of the way, speeding in every direction. Tippy was not interested in being top horse, although she was likely to have the galloping hysterics if events were not going her way. This only encouraged Mia to perform as well. The fearsome time came when I wanted to bring them in. Everybody wanted to come in first. It is a funny thing though, at turning out time they all wanted to go out first too. A horse version of FOMO? In fact, the hierarchy order was strict – Bug was always first, followed by Storm and Tippy, and then the two little Welsh ponies.

The autumn and winter continued 'unsettled', to use weather forecaster speak. My horses live out in the paddocks as much as possible – horses need to move around, socialise and graze. In those last few months of the year, even I had to give in and bring them indoors more often than usual. When the rain was horizontal and turning into sleet, healthy outdoor living was not on. My life seemed to consist of stomping through puddles, bringing excitable horses and ponies in and out of fields.

Two things happened that changed the dynamics.

Bug became ill. Bug was never a complainer. She was a tough little New Forest. Oddly, she had begun to make an excess of saliva when bridled. I bought her a hackamore, a bridle without a bit, which seemed to help. Her teeth were good for a twenty-eight-year-old. Temperature, pulse, respiration and blood tests for liver and kidney function were fine. Still, something was not right. By this time, the weather was cold, so she was stabled, just going out for a pick of grass a few times a day. One morning she took a turn for the worse. Her head was low, she was wobbly, sweaty and bleeding from her nose. Almost certainly a tumour, said the vet. It was time to say goodbye.

The second change was Storm's character. He clearly missed his Bug. His behaviour coming in and out of the field became erratic. He was seeing ghosts in the hedges and spooks in the undergrowth. More than once he got away from me completely. Bloody horse. He became more protective of Tippy – whether it was her pregnancy or losing Bug or both, I do not know – he was a complete pain. When the Fearsome Four became more hazardous than the Fearsome Five had been, I decided it was time to move Tippy to a different field, with a different companion.

Killin and Tippy lived in adjacent stables so they knew each other well. They had never been turned out together – it had not been necessary and Killin was not averse to handing out a good kicking. She had done so to Storm soon after he arrived here. Always cautious, I had her hind shoes removed and watched events carefully. I need not have worried – the two went off grazing like a couple of retired old nags. They were very peaceful in each other's company, both holding the same view that eating and sleeping are life's only concerns.

Tippy continued to take life easy. Come the spring, she seemed completely happy plodding out to the paddock with Killin by day, returning to her cool stable at night.

The summer of 2013 brought the longest heatwave since 1976. We are more aware of global temperatures rising now, in a frightening way, but back in 2013 it was considered a treat. The British in shorts and flip flops on our usually damp, windy island was a rarity. There were days on the beach, picnics on the downs and long evening rides – for some.

I was far too preoccupied with my huge mare. She could have foaled any time from 8th July onwards. Sometimes I could feel a little fluttering movement on the right-hand side of her belly. She was truly enormous, yet she could happily get down to roll in the field and the stable. She showed no sign of being in a hurry. About this time, I began doing late night and 3am checks. We tried to set up a CCTV camera from the stable to our house. It did not work. I lent it to my sister and brother-in-law to see if they could sort it. They got entertaining pictures of their dog from upstairs; that was it. The system was not strong enough for Tippy's foaling purposes. Occasionally Alanna would do the 3am check on the way home from a night out, but mostly I did not sleep for more than two hours at a time for weeks.

Tippy's due dates came and went. Expectation gave way to resignation. Tippy was never going to foal. My clients stopped asking me for news. Tippy and Killin continued munching their way through the ferociously hot days and nights of July.

The days were scorching. Harvesting was underway and everything was covered in a layer of dust. Polluted air from the continent gave the south of England its very own London smog. I had a tickly cough, itchy eyes; was exhausted, anxious and irritable.

In spite of my nightly checks, every morning I would walk to the stables, heart thumping and sick in my stomach, in case I had missed the birth and it had gone badly wrong. As I reached the yard gate, I would be greeted by a passionate neigh from Tippy – she was as hungry as a HORSE and please would I get breakfast NOW.

Late afternoon on 27th July, the weather finally broke with a massive electric storm and torrential rain. It was impressive. Lightning was flashing all around us, thunder was rolling far away, then right over our heads, then out to sea again. We all stood out in the rain in wonder, listening to the parched earth slurping it up.

I took my torch and wellies to the stable that night. I slipped Killin her slice of haylage first, as always, without shining any light. Immediately I heard deep groans from next door. It was a sound I have never heard before – almost bovine. It was nothing like the sound of a horse.

Alanna and I sat in awed silence on the mounting block outside, listening to our beloved mare heaving and groaning. She was standing up, pacing, then lying down, then getting up again. We did not interfere or disturb.

In less than ten minutes we heard a loud "Flopff!"

A beautiful filly foal had arrived, from a great height, with no trouble at all.

Chapter Eight

Tippy's story would not be complete without telling you about her eyes. Her eyes defined the first months of what should have been joyous motherhood.

A fortnight before Tippy foaled, she developed conjunctivitis, probably due to the dreadful dusty atmosphere and a weakened immune system. The vet and I were on to it straight away – she was given drops and pain relief. Because of the late stage of her pregnancy, she was not given the strongest drugs. The next day both eyes were swollen, suppurating and itchy. Tippy was rubbing them on the stable wall and had caused them to ulcerate. Stronger drugs were prescribed for her, and during the day she wore a blacked-out fly mask.

Tippy's response to the medication was erratic. There would be an improvement, then a flare-up. One eye would get better, only to become worse as the other improved. When Tippy foaled, she could barely see her baby. She could smell her, lick her, feed her and she knew where the foal was all the time, but her sight was impaired. This also made treating the eyes with drops so much more difficult as Tippy was extra protective of her baby because she could not easily see her. She could not bear to be separated from her for a second. It was a nightmare administering drops to the eyes of a distraught and bitey horse, five or six times a day. Truly, one of the most difficult tasks I have undertaken in my horsey life.

The vets wanted to take Tippy and her foal to the veterinary hospital. Family discussion revealed that none of us were happy to let Tippy and foal go. Away from home and into someone else's care? Nippy Tippy was a tricky character at the best of times. We simply could not do it. I continued with my battles to treat her. The details of her medications, numerous vet visits, eye specialist vet visit, her improvements and relapses are lengthy, so I will spare you.

Eventually, nine weeks from the outset and many hundreds of pounds later, Tippy's eyes were back to normal – big, brown, beautiful and clear. The conjunctivitis never recurred.

We called the filly Scout, after the brave little girl, Jean Louise, in Harper Lee's fabulous book *To Kill A Mockingbird*. Scout also has a pedigree name in honour of her special parents – Tippy's Shining Spark, which nobody uses but is rather lovely.

With the eyes as my priority, Scout got little attention from me. We did all the necessary things – grooming, picking out feet, putting on her foal slip, leading (or pushing) her out to the field – but I did not notice the way she was growing.

At some point after the eye episode, a vet called to see another horse and had a quick look in to admire the foal.

"My God! She is like a bullock!" she exclaimed. She wanted me to wean her straight away.

Ooh, er, really? I had not noticed her growth. I was so pleased Tippy's eyes were better and that mother and daughter were now doing so well. After all, Quarter Horses are meant to be chunky with a big backside.

Hmm. Perhaps not that big and solid at four months old.

Logistically, we could not wean Scout straight away. We began as early in the New Year as was possible. Killin had been there at the birth. She had kept close friends with Tippy throughout the pregnancy and was absolutely besotted with Scout. Time for Aunty Killin to get involved in a big way.

Weaning was easy. We have that sturdy flint wall between two paddocks. Scout went out with Killin, Tippy was separated from them by the wall. Of course, there was anxiety at first, but really nothing serious. The three could talk over the wall at any time, but Scout could not take milk. Gradually, Scout would move further away from her mother and for longer. They were stabled at night, again with a good wall between them, but they could see each other over it. Tippy stopped producing milk. By the spring they were all three living out in the big field together.

*   *   *

You would think, after all the dramas of the past twenty months, that Tippy's first summer as a mother would be a peaceful, happy time. Life is not so kind.

Now, I am not fond of mice. I know some of you love them, and you are welcome to them. They make me jump when they scuttle along the stable wall or scurry across the floor. I hate it when I reach down to pick up that last turd from the bedding and it runs away. But I can tolerate them. Live and let live. They do little harm.

Not so their bigger relatives. I cannot deal with rats. I hate them. I cannot look at them. They paralyse me with fear.

They arrive uninvited. They damage the feed sacks, make holes in the woodwork, pee on the haylage and spread disease.

Tim says, "The only good rat is a dead rat." He is wrong. Even a dead rat is terrifying.

On a happy, sunny Sunday morning, I walked down to the paddock, headcollars swinging over my shoulder, terrier dog at my side. As we approached the grassy bank near the field, there appeared to be eight baby rabbits – until SHIT! We saw their tails. Eight rats were idly sunning themselves on my grassy bank. Even the terrier turned and fled.

We have few rats on the farm. Not least because we are meticulously careful with the horse and poultry food – there is no wastage and we use no grain for the horses. Because I am so horrified by rats, I always notice if there is the slightest sign of one. One dropping – I am on it. We trap, shoot and set the (other) terrier on them.

That summer was the Year of the Rat in a big way. It was not just us. I was waiting to be served in our local agricultural store, overhearing a man telling his colleague that he had seen four hundred rats feeding outside his grain store. Four hundred! In Sussex! Where was the Pied Piper when you needed him?

I adapted my routines to minimise the chance that I might meet one face to face. I roped in help from my family, friends and pupils. It is not professional to be hiding behind a gang of thirteen-year-olds, encouraging them to make a noise, but this was an emergency. Do you know if you bounce a netball repeatedly on concrete, the rats go into hiding?

The horses were my saviours. They had no idea why I was jumpy, agitated and sometimes tearful, but they let me lead them to and from the field with my eyes shut. I would talk to Tippy and tell her all my fears as we walked. Give me a nice big horse any day.

And like this, we progressed through another anxious, unrelaxing summer. That summer and into the winter, Tim and his terrier disposed of ninety rats, on a farm which generally only has one or two. Horrifying.

If there can possibly be an upside to this tale, we have seen a massive increase in birds of prey around here. We have kestrels nesting, buzzards aplenty, regular visits from a sparrow hawk and even an occasional red kite overhead.

How I love birds of prey. We have not had a similar rat infestation since.

Chapter Nine

Watching the three horses living as a family was enchanting. Tippy was gentle and soft interacting with her daughter – moving her along with a nudge, nuzzling her, telling her off and keeping her safe. It was perfect, unconditional love both ways – a whole new experience for Tippy.

Killin, too, was a devoted aunty. As you know, Killin could be a bit of a bully to the other horses. Not with this young foal. She watched the youngster's every move and tolerated all manner of bouncy foal play. Occasionally there would be a mass chasing game. All three would set off around the field at a gallop – the Quarter Horses slicing up the turf in a way that no Thoroughbred can. Not good for the field but exhilarating to watch.

When Scout went to share Killin's food, Killin would squeal and put her ears back, but never chase her away. To this day, I do not think Scout knows what 'ears back' means. After all, her mum does it all the time and nothing bad happens.

Tippy was always going to be a slightly eccentric mother. She was still prone to having the galloping hysterics if the weather suddenly turned bad, or supper was late, or the midges were biting. The other two would watch her in bemusement from their place standing by the gate. Aunty Killin was a wonderfully calming influence on young Scout.

Sometimes it was all a bit too cuddly and close. They would walk into each other, oblivious of personal space, and no one seemed to mind. When I was leading or grooming, I was treated in much the same way – often squashed between them in a loving 'Quarter Horse sandwich'. They were very gentle – I was just another member of the herd. What an honour.

By the time Scout was four years old, Killin was quite a creaky old lady, and it had become apparent that she was not lying down as often as she should. She was not getting muddy in the field, nor covered in bedding in the stable. This was not because she could not get down, it was because getting up was difficult. Her hind legs were losing power. The dreaded day came when she gave up trying. On a beautiful crisp autumn morning, I had bought Tippy and Scout in from the field together as usual. Killin bought herself in, as was her habit, nibbling a bit of grass on route. She had her breakfast and then I was pleased to see her have a lie down. An hour later, she was still down. Although she made a little effort to get up, she had no strength in those hind legs and quickly gave up. She could not do it.

The strongest instinct a horse has is to gallop away from fear and danger. To see a once proud and strong horse unable to put that instinct into action is a terrible thing. We may well have been able to haul her up with ropes and brute strength. But for what? To see her suffer this again, on another day?

Tippy and Scout were in the adjacent stable watching over the wall at events unfolding. After the vet had put

Killin to sleep, I let them both come in to see her. Scout spent a long time sniffing her and gave her a good licking. That evening, when Tippy and Scout went out in the field, just the two of them, there was no neighing, no distress. They knew exactly what had happened to Aunty and understood the time was right.

*   *   *

Tippy is twenty now, but you would not guess it. Only a slight greying on her eyebrows gives a clue. She is plump and curvy, having spent twelve weeks off work due to the Covid-19 lockdown. Unlike most of us, Tippy thought lockdown was the best thing. She always said social distancing was the way forward and self-isolating with one family member was a pleasure.

The riding school reopened recently with many new regulations and fewer pupils at the school at any one time.

Again, just what Tippy has always had in mind.

She is a content and happy horse. No broncoing, no biting. She only grinds and clunks her teeth occasionally when she remembers she has a reputation to keep up.

During lockdown, Alanna wrote a poem for Tippy. She understands our beautiful, enigmatic, dark horse perfectly. With her permission, I am using the poem to close Tippy's Story:

The Quarter-mile.

We bought a Quarter Horse with a cocktail name
when I was younger.
She was chocolate brown with high cheekbones
and had a terrible temper.

She bit me badly once—
left a perfect round hole in my stomach
where you could see the fat.

I tried to hide it
in case it meant we couldn't keep her,
but she stayed and we put a sign up
'Keep away.'

When she was herself a young girl,
she'd had a rough time in the show circuit
and it had turned her cross.

I imagined that if people circled me,
critiquing my looks,
I'd bare my teeth at them too.

But when no one was looking, in the dusty stable,
her sleepy eyes would close,
and sometimes I'd catch her dreaming.

I remembered that people say
you are who you are when no one is watching.
Sweet girl.

After some years with us, I found something out
    about her.
Quarter Horses are named such
because they are the fastest horse in the world
over a quarter of a mile.

So, I told her, no more show cages:
me, you and the Wild West.
I curled up on her back and she flew
like five claps of thunder.

A speed that could never be taught or won.

After, when I dismounted,
she lowered her large head into my lap—
nothing but soft lips.

And I understood,
sometimes, to earn someone's trust,
you must gallop a quarter-mile in their shoes.

About the author

Lucy Postgate's horse riding career began as a young child playing ponies cantering around her London bedroom. After the family moved to East Sussex Lucy began to learn to ride real ponies at Hope in the Valley Riding School in Lewes. She was aged ten. Lucy went on to take and pass her BHSAI in 1975 and has been running her own riding school since 1977. Lucy is married to Tim Duffield. They have two grown-up children, George and Alanna.

9 781839 754531